Summary

The causes of homelessness and determining how best to assist those who find themselves homeless became particularly prominent, visible issues in the 1980s. The concept of homelessness may seem like a straightforward one, with individuals and families who have no place to live falling within the definition. However, the extent of homelessness in this country and how best to address it depend upon how one defines the condition of being homeless.

There is no single federal definition of homelessness, although a number of programs, including those overseen by the Department of Housing and Urban Development (HUD), Department of Veterans Affairs (VA), Department of Homeland Security (DHS), and Department of Labor (DOL) use the definition enacted as part of the McKinney-Vento Homeless Assistance Act (P.L. 100-77). The McKinney-Vento Act definition of a homeless individual was recently broadened as part of the Helping Families Save Their Homes Act of 2009 (P.L. 111-22). Previously, a homeless individual was defined as a person who lacks a fixed nighttime residence and whose primary nighttime residence is a supervised public or private shelter designed to provide temporary living accommodations, a facility accommodating persons intended to be institutionalized, or a place not intended to be used as a regular sleeping accommodation for human beings. The new law expanded the definition to include those defined as homeless under other federal programs, in certain circumstances, as well as those who will imminently lose housing. In the 112th Congress, a bill that would further expand the McKinney-Vento Act definition, the Homeless Children and Youth Act of 2011 (H.R. 32), has been approved by the House Financial Services Committee, Subcommittee on Insurance, Housing and Community Opportunity.

A number of federal programs in seven different agencies, many originally authorized by the McKinney-Vento Act, serve homeless persons. These include the Education for Homeless Children and Youth program administered by the Department of Education (ED) and the Emergency Food and Shelter program, a Federal Emergency Management Agency (FEMA) program run by the Department of Homeland Security. The Department of Health and Human Services (HHS) administers multiple programs that serve homeless individuals, including Health Care for the Homeless, Projects for Assistance in Transition from Homelessness, and the Runaway and Homeless Youth program.

HUD administers the Homeless Assistance Grants, made up of grant programs that provide housing and services for homeless individuals ranging from emergency shelter to permanent housing. The VA operates numerous programs that serve homeless veterans. These include Health Care for Homeless Veterans and the Homeless Providers Grant and Per Diem program, as well as a collaborative program with HUD called HUD-VASH, through which homeless veterans receive Section 8 vouchers from HUD and supportive services through the VA. The Department of Labor also operates a program for homeless veterans, the Homeless Veterans Reintegration Program.

This report describes the federal programs that are targeted to assist those who are homeless; includes recent funding levels (see **Table 1** and **Table 2**); discusses current issues, including homelessness after the economic downturn and federal efforts to end homelessness; and provides information on recent legislation. Among active legislation are bills to reauthorize the Violence Against Women Act, which includes transitional housing for those who are homeless as a result of domestic violence (S. 1925 and H.R. 4970) and legislation that would, among other things, reauthorize the Education for Homeless Children and Youth program (H.R. 3989 and H.R. 3990).

Contents

Tables

Contacts

Introduction

Federal assistance targeted to homeless individuals and families was largely nonexistent prior to the mid-1980s. Although the Runaway and Homeless Youth program was enacted in 1974 as part of the Juvenile Justice and Delinquency Prevention Act (P.L. 93-415), the first federal program focused on assisting all homeless people, no matter their age, was the Emergency Food and Shelter (EFS) program, established in March 1983 through an emergency jobs appropriation bill (P.L. 98-8). The EFS program was and continues to be administered by the Federal Emergency Management Agency (FEMA) in the Department of Homeland Security (DHS) to provide emergency food and shelter to needy individuals.

In 1987, Congress enacted the Stewart B. McKinney Homeless Assistance Act (P.L. 100-77), which created a number of new programs to comprehensively address the needs of homeless people, including food, shelter, health care, and education. The act was later renamed the McKinney-Vento Homeless Assistance Act (P.L. 106-400) after its two prominent proponents— Representatives Stewart B. McKinney and Bruce F. Vento. The programs authorized in McKinney-Vento include the Department of Housing and Urban Development (HUD) Homeless Assistance Grants, the Department of Labor (DOL) Homeless Veterans Reintegration Program, the Department of Health and Human Services (HHS) Grants for the Benefit of Homeless Individuals and Health Care for the Homeless, and the Department of Education (ED) Education for Homeless Children and Youths program.

This report describes existing federal programs that provide targeted assistance to homeless individuals and families (other federal programs may provide assistance to homeless individuals but are not specifically designed to assist homeless persons). These include those programs listed above, as well as others that Congress has created since the enactment of McKinney-Vento. In addition, this report discusses current issues related to homelessness, including the recent economic downturn and federal efforts to end homelessness. Finally, **Table 1** at the end of this report shows funding levels for each of the ED, DHS, HHS, HUD, DOL, and Department of Justice (DOJ) programs that assist homeless individuals. **Table 2** shows funding levels for VA programs.

The Federal Response to Homelessness

Homelessness in the United States has always existed, but it did not come to the public's attention as a national issue until the 1970s and 1980s, when the characteristics of the homeless population and their living arrangements began to change. Throughout the early and middle part of the 20th century, homelessness was typified by "skid rows": areas with hotels and single-room occupancy dwellings where transient single men lived.[1] Skid rows were usually removed from the more populated areas of cities, and it was uncommon for individuals to actually live on the streets.[2] Beginning in the 1970s, however, the homeless population began to grow and become more visible to the general public. According to studies from the time, homeless persons were no longer almost exclusively single men, but included women with children; their median age was

---

[1] Peter H. Rossi, *Down and Out in America: The Origins of Homelessness* (Chicago: The University of Chicago Press, 1989), pp. 20-21, 27-28.

[2] Ibid., p. 34.

younger; they were more racially diverse (in previous decades, the observed homeless population was largely white); they were less likely to be employed (and therefore had lower incomes); they were mentally ill in higher proportions than previously; and individuals who were abusing or had abused drugs began to become more prevalent in the population.[3]

A number of reasons have been offered for the growth in the number of homeless persons and their increasing visibility. Many cities demolished skid rows to make way for urban development, leaving some residents without affordable housing options.[4] Other possible factors contributing to homelessness include the decreased availability of affordable housing generally, the reduced need for seasonal unskilled labor, the reduced likelihood that relatives will accommodate homeless family members, the decreased value of public benefits, and changed admissions standards at mental hospitals.[5] The increased visibility of homeless people was due, in part, to the decriminalization of actions such as public drunkenness, loitering, and vagrancy.[6]

In the 1980s, Congress first responded to the growing prevalence of homelessness with several separate grant programs designed to address the food and shelter needs of homeless individuals. These programs included the Emergency Food and Shelter Program (P.L. 98-8), the Emergency Shelter Grants Program (P.L. 99-591), and the Transitional Housing Demonstration Program (P.L. 99-591).[7] In 1983, the first federal task force was created to provide information to local governments and other parties on how to obtain surplus federal property that could be used for providing shelter and other services for homeless persons.

Congress began to consider comprehensive legislation to address homelessness in 1986. On June 26, 1986, H.R. 5140 and S. 2608 were introduced as the Homeless Persons' Survival Act to provide an aid package for homeless persons. No further action was taken on either measure, however. Later that same year, legislation containing Title I of the Homeless Persons' Survival Act—emergency relief provisions for shelter, food, mobile health care, and transitional housing—was introduced as the Urgent Relief for the Homeless Act (H.R. 5710). The legislation passed both houses of Congress in 1987 with large bipartisan majorities. The act was renamed the Stewart B. McKinney Homeless Assistance Act after the death of its chief sponsor, Stewart B. McKinney of Connecticut; it was renamed again on October 30, 2000, as the McKinney-Vento Homeless Assistance Act after the death of another prominent sponsor, Bruce F. Vento of Minnesota. In 1987, President Ronald Reagan signed the act into law (P.L. 100-77).

The original version of the McKinney-Vento Act consisted of 15 programs either created or reauthorized by the act, providing an array of services for homeless persons and administered by various federal agencies. The act also established the Interagency Council on Homelessness, which is designed to provide guidance on the federal response to homelessness through the coordination of the efforts of multiple federal agencies covered under the McKinney-Vento Act. Since the enactment of the McKinney-Vento Homeless Assistance Act, there have been some legislative changes to programs and services provided under the act and new programs that target

---

[3] Ibid., pp. 39-44.

[4] Ibid., p. 33.

[5] Ibid., pp. 181-194, 41. See also Martha Burt, *Over the Edge: The Growth of Homelessness in the 1980s* (New York: Russell Sage Foundation, 1992), pp. 31-126.

[6] Down and Out in America, p. 34; Over the Edge, p. 123.

[7] All three programs were incorporated into the McKinney-Vento Homeless Assistance Act in 1987. (The Transitional Housing Demonstration Program was renamed the Supportive Housing Demonstration Program.)

homeless individuals have been created. Specific programs covered under the McKinney-Vento Act, as well as other federal programs responding to homelessness, are discussed in this report.

Defining Homelessness: Who Is Served

There is no single federal definition of what it means to be homeless, and definitions among federal programs that serve homeless individuals may vary to some degree. As a result, the populations served through the federal programs described in this report may differ depending on the program. The definition of "homeless individual" that was originally enacted in the McKinney-Vento Act is used by a majority of programs to define what it means to be homeless. The McKinney-Vento Act defined the term "homeless individual" for purposes of the programs that were authorized through the law (see Section 103 of McKinney-Vento), though some programs that were originally authorized through McKinney-Vento use their own, less restrictive definitions.[8] In 2009, the McKinney-Vento Act definition of homelessness was amended by the Homeless Emergency Assistance and Rapid Transition to Housing (HEARTH) Act, enacted as part of the Helping Families Save Their Homes Act (P.L. 111-22).

Programs that use the definition in Section 103 of the McKinney-Vento Act are HUD's Homeless Assistance Grants, FEMA's Emergency Food and Shelter program, the VA homeless veterans programs, and DOL's Homeless Veterans Reintegration Program.[9] (Throughout this section of the report, the term "Section 103 definition" is used to refer to the original McKinney-Vento Act definition of homelessness.)

This section describes the original McKinney-Vento Act Section 103 definition of homeless individual, how the definition compares to those used in other programs, how it has changed under the HEARTH Act and HUD's implementing regulations, and how a bill in the 112th Congress, the Homeless Children and Youth Act of 2012 (H.R. 32), would further change the definition.

Original McKinney-Vento Act Definition of Homelessness

The definition of the term "homeless individual" in Section 103 of McKinney-Vento remained the same for years, defining a homeless individual as

> [a]n individual who lacks a fixed, regular, and adequate nighttime residence; and a person who has a nighttime residence that is (a) a supervised publicly or privately operated shelter designed to provide temporary living accommodations (including welfare hotels, congregate shelters, and transitional housing for the mentally ill); (b) an institution that provides a temporary residence for individuals intended to be institutionalized; or (c) a public or private place not designed for, nor ordinarily used as, a regular sleeping accommodation for human beings.

---

[8] These include the Education for Homeless Children and Youths program and Health Care for the Homeless.

[9] The definition of *homeless veteran* is a veteran who is homeless as defined by McKinney-Vento. 38 U.S.C. §2002(1). This definition applies to VA programs for homeless veterans as well as the Homeless Veterans Reintegration Program.

This definition was sometimes described as requiring one to be literally homeless in order to meet its requirements[10]—either living in emergency accommodations or having no place to stay. This contrasts with definitions used in some other federal programs, where a person may currently have a place to live but is still considered to be homeless because the accommodation is precarious or temporary.

Definitions Under Other Federal Programs

Education for Homeless Children and Youths: Among the federal programs that have adopted a definition of homelessness that differs from the Section 103 definition is the Department of Education (ED) Education for Homeless Children and Youths program. The ED program defines homeless children and youth in part by reference to the Section 103 definition of homeless individuals as those lacking a fixed, regular, and adequate nighttime residence.[11] In addition, however, the ED program defines children and youth who are eligible for services to include those who are (1) sharing housing with other persons due to loss of housing or economic hardship; (2) living in hotels or motels, trailer parks, or campgrounds due to lack of alternative arrangements; (3) awaiting foster care placement; (4) living in substandard housing; and (5) children of migrant workers.[12]

Transitional Housing Assistance for Victims of Domestic Violence, Stalking, or Sexual Assault: The Violence Against Women Act definition of homelessness is similar to the ED definition.[13]

Runaway and Homeless Youth: The statute defines a homeless youth as either ages 16 to 22 (for transitional housing) or ages 18 and younger (for short-term shelter) and for whom it is not possible to live in a safe environment with a relative or for whom there is no other safe alternative living arrangement.[14]

Health Care for the Homeless: Under the Health Care for the Homeless program, a homeless individual is one who "lacks housing," and the definition includes those living in a private or publicly operated temporary living facility or in transitional housing.[15]

Projects for Assistance in Transition from Homelessness: In the PATH program, an "eligible homeless individual" is described as one suffering from serious mental illness, which may also be accompanied by a substance use disorder, and who is "homeless or at imminent risk of becoming homeless." The statute does not further define what constitutes being homeless or at imminent risk of homelessness, however.

---

[10] See, for example, the Department of Housing and Urban Development, *The Third Annual Homeless Assessment Report to Congress*, July 2008, p. 2, footnote 5, http://www.hudhre.info/documents/3rdHomelessAssessmentReport.pdf.

[11] 42 U.S.C. §11434a.

[12] Migratory children are defined at 20 U.S.C. §6399.

[13] 42 U.S.C. §14043e-2.

[14] 42 U.S.C. §5732a(3).

[15] 42 U.S.C. §254b(h)(5)(A).

HEARTH Act Changes to the McKinney-Vento Act Section 103 Definition

The Section 103 definition of "homeless individual" was changed in 2009 as part of the Homeless Emergency Assistance and Rapid Transition to Housing (HEARTH) Act, enacted as part of the Helping Families Save Their Homes Act (P.L. 111-22). The HEARTH Act broadened the McKinney-Vento Section 103 definition and moved the definition away from the requirement for literal homelessness. On December 5, 2011, HUD released regulations that clarify some of the changes.[16] The changes are as follows:

- **Amendments to Original McKinney-Vento Act Language:** The HEARTH Act made minor changes to the existing language in the McKinney-Vento Act. The law continues to provide that a person is homeless if they lack "a fixed, regular, and adequate nighttime residence," and if their nighttime residence is a place not meant for human habitation, if they live in a shelter, or if they are a person leaving an institution who had been homeless prior to being institutionalized. The HEARTH Act added that those living in hotels or motels paid for by a government entity or charitable organization are considered homeless, and it included all those persons living in transitional housing, not just those residing in transitional housing for the mentally ill as in prior law. The amended law also added circumstances that are not considered suitable places for people to sleep, including cars, parks, abandoned buildings, bus or train stations, airports, and campgrounds. When HUD issued its final regulation in December 2011, it clarified that a person exiting an institution cannot have been residing there for more than 90 days.[17] In addition, where the law states that a person "who resided in a shelter or place not meant for human habitation" prior to institutionalization, the "shelter" means emergency shelter and does not include transitional housing.[18]

- **Imminent Loss of Housing:** P.L. 111-22 added to the Section 103 definition those individuals and families who meet all of the following criteria:

  - They will "imminently lose their housing," whether it be their own housing, housing they are sharing with others, or a hotel or motel not paid for by a government or charitable entity. Imminent loss of housing is evidenced by an eviction requiring an individual or family to leave their housing within 14 days; a lack of resources that would allow an individual or family to remain in a hotel or motel for more than 14 days; or credible evidence that an individual or family would not be able to stay with another homeowner or renter for more than 14 days.

  - They have no subsequent residence identified.

  - They lack the resources or support networks needed to obtain other permanent housing.

---

[16] U.S. Department of Housing and Urban Development, "Homeless Emergency Assistance and Rapid Transition to Housing: Defining 'Homeless'," 76 *Federal Register* 75994-76019, December 5, 2011.

[17] Ibid., p. 76000.

[18] Ibid.

HUD practice prior to passage of the HEARTH Act was to consider those individuals and families who would imminently lose housing within seven days to be homeless.

- **Other Federal Definitions:** P.L. 111-22 added to the definition of "homeless individual" unaccompanied youth and homeless families with children who are defined as homeless under other federal statutes. The law did not define the term youth, so in its final regulations HUD defined a youth as someone under the age of 25.[19] In addition, the HEARTH Act did not specify which other federal statutes would be included in defining homeless families with children and unaccompanied youth. So in its regulations, HUD listed seven federal programs as those under which youth or families with children can be defined as homeless: the Runaway and Homeless Youth program; Head Start; the Violence Against Women Act; the Health Care for the Homeless program; the Supplemental Nutrition Assistance Program (SNAP); the Women, Infants, and Children nutrition program; and the McKinney-Vento Education for Children and Youths program.[20] Five of these seven programs (all but Runaway and Homeless Youth and Health Care for the Homeless programs) either share the Education for Homeless Children and Youths definition, or use a very similar definition. Youth and families who are defined as homeless under another federal program must meet each of the following criteria:

  - They have experienced a long-term period without living independently in permanent housing. In its final regulation, HUD defined "long-term period" to mean at least 60 days.

  - They have experienced instability as evidenced by frequent moves during this long-term period, defined by HUD to mean at least two moves during the 60 days prior to applying for assistance.[21]

  - The youth or families with children can be expected to continue in unstable housing due to factors such as chronic disabilities, chronic physical health or mental health conditions, substance addiction, histories of domestic violence or childhood abuse, the presence of a child or youth with a disability, or multiple barriers to employment. Under the final regulation, barriers to employment may include the lack of a high school degree, illiteracy, lack of English proficiency, a history of incarceration, or a history of unstable employment.[22]

  HUD Homeless Assistance Grant recipients will not be able to use more than 10% of grant funds to serve those individuals and families defined as homeless under other federal statutes.[23]

- **Domestic Violence:** Another change to the definition of homeless individual is that the HEARTH Act considers homeless anyone who is fleeing a situation of

---

[19] Ibid., p. 75996.

[20] Ibid.

[21] Ibid., p. 76017.

[22] Ibid.

[23] 42 U.S.C. §11382(j).

"domestic violence, dating violence, sexual assault, stalking, or other dangerous or life-threatening conditions in the individual's or family's current housing situation, including where the health and safety of children are jeopardized."[24] The law also provides that an individual must lack the resources or support network to find another housing situation. The final regulation issued by HUD in December 2011 specified that the conditions either must have occurred at the primary nighttime residence or made the individual or family afraid to return to their residence.[25]

Legislation in the 112ᵗʰ Congress Regarding the Definition of Homelessness

The Homeless Children and Youth Act of 2011 (H.R. 32) would further change the McKinney-Vento Section 103 definition of homelessness, as amended by the HEARTH Act, to include children and youth who are verified as homeless using the definitions of four other federal programs. Specifically, youth verified as homeless under the Runaway and Homeless Youth program, and children and their families verified as homeless under (1) the Education for Homeless Children and Youths program, (2) programs funded through the Individuals with Disabilities Education Act (IDEA), or (3) Head Start would meet the Section 103 definition of homelessness. Note that both IDEA and Head Start refer to the Department of Education statute to define "homeless children."[26]

The proposed changes in H.R. 32 differ from HEARTH Act changes in that the verification of homelessness under one of the four federal programs would be sufficient to qualify as homeless under the McKinney-Vento Section 103 definition. Children and their families and youth would not need to demonstrate housing instability, together with factors that would prevent achieving housing stability, as is required under the HEARTH Act. Children or youth would be verified by local education agency homeless liaisons (in the case of the ED program), and the directors of Head Start, Runaway and Homeless Youth, and IDEA programs, or their designees.

Federal Programs Targeted to Assist Homeless Individuals

The following subsections describe each of the federal programs targeted to assist homeless individuals, arranged by the agency administering the programs. Where relevant, there are references to other CRS reports that go into more detail about the programs.

---

[24] 42 U.S.C. §11302(b).

[25] 76 *Federal Register*, p. 76014.

[26] See 20 U.S.C. §1401 and 42 U.S.C. §9832.

Department of Education (ED)

Education for Homeless Children and Youths

(42 U.S.C. §§11431-11435) This program was initially authorized under Title VII, Part B, of the McKinney-Vento Homeless Assistance Act; it provides assistance to state educational agencies (SEAs) to ensure that all homeless children and youth have equal access to the same free, appropriate public education, including public preschool education, that is provided to other children and youth. Grants made by SEAs to local educational agencies (LEAs) under this program must be used to facilitate the enrollment, attendance, and success in school of homeless children and youth. The LEAs may use the funds for activities such as tutoring, supplemental instruction, and referral services for homeless children and youth, as well as providing them with medical, dental, mental, and other health services. In order to receive funds, each state must submit a plan indicating how homeless children and youth will be identified, how assurances will be put in place that homeless children will participate in federal, state, and local food programs if eligible, and how the state will address such problems as transportation, immunization, residency requirements, and the lack of birth certificates or school records.

Education for Homeless Children and Youth Program (EHCY) grants are allotted to SEAs in proportion to grants made under Title I, Part A of the Elementary and Secondary Education Act of 1965 (ESEA), except that no state can receive less than the greater of $150,000, 0.25% of the total annual appropriation, or the amount received in FY2001 under this program. The Department of Education must reserve 0.1% of the total appropriation in order to provide grants to outlying areas (Virgin Islands, Guam, American Samoa, and the Commonwealth of the Northern Mariana Islands). The department must also transfer 1.0% of the total appropriation to the Department of the Interior for services to homeless children and youth provided by the Bureau of Indian Education. States may reserve up to 25% of their Homeless Education program funding for state activities. Minimally funded states (defined as states that receive a Homeless Education allocation in a fiscal year equal to 0.25% of total program funds for that fiscal year) are permitted to reserve up to 50% of funding for state activities. States subsequently subgrant remaining funds to LEAs competitively.

Not all LEAs receive EHCY grants. In school year (SY) 2009-2010, 3,046 LEAs, out of a total of 15,906, received awards. Although only 19% percent of LEAs received EHCY grants in SY2009-2010, they enrolled 80% of all homeless students in that year. All LEAs are required to report data annually on the number of homeless students enrolled, regardless of whether or not they receive a McKinney-Vento Homeless Education grant. All data are reported based on a school year. In SY2007-2008, 794,617 homeless students were reported enrolled in school; in SY2008-2009, 956,914 homeless students were reported enrolled; and in SY2009-2010, the number of enrolled homeless students reported was 939,903. The total number of homeless students enrolled increased by 21% between SY2007-2008 and SY2008-2009, but it declined by 2% between SY2008-2009 and SY2009-2010. This decline was due in part to changes in data collection procedures in California. If California were excluded from the total, there would have been an increase of 11% in enrolled homeless students between SY2008-2009 and SY2009-2010. Four states accounted for 43% of the total number of students enrolled in both LEAs with EHCY subgrants and those without in SY2009-2010. Those states, and their percentages of total homeless student enrollment, were California (21%), New York (9%), Texas (8.5%), and Florida (5%).

The most recent reauthorization of the ESEA, known as the No Child Left Behind Act of 2001 (P.L. 107-110), amended the program explicitly to prohibit states that receive McKinney-Vento funds from segregating homeless students from non-homeless students, except for short periods of time for health and safety emergencies or to provide temporary, special, supplementary services.[27] EHCY was reauthorized through FY2007 as Title X, Part C of the No Child Left Behind Act of 2001 (FY2008 with the automatic one-year extension provided by the General Education Provisions Act).[28] The Housing and Economic Recovery Act of 2008, signed into law on July 30, 2008 (P.L. 110-289), increased the authorization for EHCY from $70 million to $100 million for FY2009, and such sums as may be necessary for each subsequent fiscal year. (For more information about the Education for Homeless Children and Youth Program, see CRS Report R42494, *Education for Homeless Children and Youth: Background and Legislation in the 112th Congress*, by Gail McCallion.)

Department of Homeland Security (DHS)

Emergency Food and Shelter (EFS) Program

(42 U.S.C. §§11331-11352) The Emergency Food and Shelter program, the oldest federal program serving all homeless populations,[29] was established in March 1983 and is administered by the Federal Emergency Management Agency (FEMA), in the Department of Homeland Security. The program allocates funds to local communities to fund homeless programs and homelessness prevention services. The EFS program is governed by a National Board chaired by FEMA and made up of representatives from the United Way Worldwide, the Salvation Army, the National Council of Churches of Christ in the U.S.A., Catholic Charities U.S.A., United Jewish Communities, and the American Red Cross. The National Board uses a formula comprised of unemployment rates and poverty rates to determine which local jurisdictions (typically counties) qualify for funds. Eligible local jurisdictions then convene a local board to determine which organizations—nonprofits and government agencies—within their communities should receive grants, and distribute their available funds accordingly.[30]

Eligible expenses for which local organizations may use funds include items for food pantries such as groceries, food vouchers, and transportation expenses related to the delivery of food; items for mass shelters such as hot meals, transportation of clients to shelters or food service providers, and toiletries; payments to prevent homelessness such as utility assistance, hotel or motel lodging, rental or mortgage assistance, and first month's rent; and local recipient organization program expenses such as building maintenance or repair, and equipment purchases up to $300.

The EFS program was established by the Temporary Emergency Food Assistance Act of 1983 (P.L. 98-8); in 1987 it was authorized under the McKinney-Vento Homeless Assistance Act. The

---

[27] An exception was made for four counties that operated separate schools for homeless students in FY2000 (San Joaquin, Orange, and San Diego counties in California, and Maricopa County in Arizona), as long as (1) those separate schools offer services that are comparable to local schools, and (2) homeless children are not required to attend them.

[28] See Section 422 of the General Education Provisions Act, as amended by P.L. 103-382. 42 U.S.C. §1226a.

[29] Another program, the Runaway and Homeless Youth Program, was enacted earlier than the Emergency Food and Shelter Program (in 1974), but serves a specific population rather than all homeless persons generally.

[30] For more information about recipient jurisdictions, see the National Board website, http://efsp.unitedway.org/.

authorization for the EFS program expired at the end of FY1994 (42 U.S.C. §11352), however it continues to be funded through annual appropriations.

Department of Health and Human Services (HHS)

Health Care for the Homeless (HCH) Program

(42 U.S.C. §254b(h)) The Health Care for the Homeless (HCH) Program provides grants to nonprofit, state, or local government entities to operate outpatient health centers for homeless individuals. It is one of the four types of health centers authorized in Section 330 of the Public Health Service Act (42 U.S.C. §§201 et. seq.). The HCH is the only federal program that focuses on the health care needs of the homeless population. Centers funded under the HCH are required to be community designed and operated and must provide primary health care and substance abuse prevention and treatment services to homeless individuals. Centers may also provide services to connect homeless individuals with support services such as emergency shelter and job training and may provide care at mobile sites. Finally, the HCH program authorizes grants to fund innovative programs that provide outreach and comprehensive primary health services to homeless children and children at risk of homelessness. In 2010, there were 2,438 HCH sites that provided care to 805,0694 homeless individuals. The vast majority of these patients (over 90%) lived at or below the federal poverty level, and approximately 15% of the patients served were under the age of 20.[31] HCHs were permanently authorized in the Patient Protection and Affordable Care Act (P.L. 111-148). (For more information about health centers, see CRS Report R42433, *Federal Health Centers*, by Elayne J. Heisler.)

Projects for Assistance in Transition from Homelessness (PATH)

(42 U.S.C. §290cc-21 through §290cc-35) Projects for Assistance in Transition from Homelessness (PATH) is a formula grant program that distributes funds to states (including the 50 states, the District of Columbia, Puerto Rico, Guam, the U.S. Virgin Islands, American Samoa, and the Northern Mariana Islands) to support local organizations providing services for people with serious mental illness (including those with co-occurring substance use disorders) who are homeless or at imminent risk of becoming homeless. Funds are distributed to states in amounts proportional to their populations living in urbanized areas; the minimum allotment is $300,000 for each of the 50 states, the District of Columbia, and Puerto Rico, and $50,000 for each of the other territories. States must provide matching funds of at least $1 for every $3 of federal funds. Up to 20% of the federal payments may be used for housing-related assistance, including (but not limited to) services to help individuals access housing, minor repairs, security deposits, and one-time rental payments to prevent eviction. Other services include (but are not limited to) outreach, mental health and substance abuse treatment, case management, and job training. Administered by the Substance Abuse and Mental Health Services Administration's (SAMHSA's) Center for Mental Health Services (within HHS), PATH grants currently support services in 483 communities.[32] Authorization for the PATH program expired at the end of FY2003; however, it continues to be funded through annual appropriations.

---

[31] HRSA, Uniform Data System (UDS) Report, UDS, National Rollup Report, 2010, at http://bphc.hrsa.gov/uds/doc/2010/National_Universal.pdf; and National Total Summary Data at http://bphc hrsa.gov/uds/view.aspx?year=2010.

[32] SAMHSA, *FY2013 Justification of Estimates for Appropriations Committees*, p. 71, http://www.samhsa.gov/Budget/ (continued...)

Grants for the Benefit of Homeless Individuals

(42 U.S.C. §290aa-5) Grants for the Benefit of Homeless Individuals (GBHI) is a competitive grant program that supports services to homeless individuals with substance use disorders (including those with co-occurring mental illness). Grants are awarded competitively to community-based public or nonprofit entities for periods of up to five years. GBHI-funded programs and services including substance abuse treatment, mental health services, wrap-around services, immediate entry into treatment, outreach services, screening and diagnostic services, staff training, case management, primary health services, job training, educational services, and relevant housing services. Administered by the SAMHSA's Center for Substance Abuse Treatment, GBHI funds have served 49,300 individuals; the currently active portfolio has served over 13,500 individuals.[33] Authorization for the GBHI program expired at the end of FY2003; however, it continues to be funded through annual appropriations.

Runaway and Homeless Youth Program

The Runaway and Homeless Youth Program is administered by the Family and Youth Services Bureau (FYSB) within HHS's Administration for Children and Families (ACF). The program was established in 1974 and was most recently authorized by the Reconnecting Homeless Youth Act of 2008 (P.L. 110-378). The law authorizes federal funding for three programs through FY2013: the Basic Center Program (BCP), Transitional Living Program (TLP), and Street Outreach Program (SOP). These programs are designed to provide services to runaway and homeless youth outside of the law enforcement, juvenile justice, child welfare, and mental health systems. The funding streams for the Basic Center Program and Transitional Living Program were separate until Congress consolidated them in 1999 (P.L. 106-71). Together, the two programs, along with other program activities, are known as the Consolidated Runaway and Homeless Youth Program.[34] Although the Street Outreach Program is a separately funded component, SOP services are coordinated with those provided under the BCP and TLP. Grantees must provide at least 10% of the funds to cover the total cost of the services provided under the three programs. (For more information about the program, see CRS Report RL33785, *Runaway and Homeless Youth: Demographics and Programs*, by Adrienne L. Fernandes-Alcantara.)

Basic Center Program

(42 U.S.C. §§5701-5751) The Basic Center Program is intended to provide short-term shelter and services for youth under age 18 and their families through public and private community-based centers. Youth eligible to receive BCP services include those youth who are at risk of running away or becoming homeless (and who may live at home with their parents), or have already left home, either voluntarily or involuntarily. These centers, which generally shelter as many as 20 youth for approximately two weeks, are located in areas that are frequented or easily reached by

---

(...continued)

FY2013/SAMHSAFY2013CJ.pdf.

[33] Ibid., p. 129.

[34] Other program activities include a national communications system for runaway youth and their families, logistical support for grantee organizations, HHS's National Clearinghouse on Families and Youth, demonstrations, and the administration of the management information system that tracks data on runaway and homeless youth, known as NEO-RHYMIS.

runaway and homeless youth. The centers seek to reunite youth with their families, whenever possible, or to locate appropriate alternative placements. The centers also provide food, clothing, individual and family counseling, and health care referrals. Some centers serve homeless youth ages 18 to 21 through street-based services, home-based services, and drug abuse education and prevention services.

BCP grants are allocated by formula to each state, the District of Columbia, and Puerto Rico, and are then distributed by HHS on a competitive basis to community-based organizations. The amount of BCP funding available to a jurisdiction is based on its proportion of the nation's youth under age 18, and under the law, each jurisdiction receives a minimum of $200,000. Separately, each of the territories (U.S. Virgin Islands, Guam, America Samoa, and the Northern Mariana Islands) receives a minimum of $70,000 of the total appropriations.[35] Grantees are required to establish relationships with law enforcement, health and mental health care, social service, welfare, and school district systems to coordinate services.

Transitional Living Program

(42 U.S.C. §5714-1 through §5714-2) The Transitional Living Program provides longer-term shelter and assistance for youth ages 16 through 22 (including pregnant and/or parenting youth) who may leave their biological homes due to family conflict, or have left and are not expected to return home. TLP grants are distributed competitively by HHS to community-based public and private organizations. Each TLP grantee may shelter up to 20 youth at host family homes, supervised apartments owned by a social service agency, or scattered-site apartments and single-occupancy apartments rented directly with the assistance of the agency. Youth under age 18 may remain at TLP projects for up to 540 days (18 months) or longer. Youth ages 16 through 22 may remain in the program for a continuous period of 635 days (approximately 21 months) under "exceptional circumstances."[36] Youth receive several types of TLP services:

- basic life-skills training, including consumer education, and instruction in budgeting and housekeeping;

- interpersonal skill-building;

- educational preparation, such as GED courses and post-secondary training;

- assistance in job preparation and attainment;

- education and counseling on substance abuse; and

- mental and physical health care services.

The 2003 amendments to the Runaway, Homeless, and Missing Children Protection Act (P.L. 108-96) provided statutory authority for TLP funds to be used for maternity group homes. Grantees may and do use TLP funds to directly serve unwed pregnant and parenting teens, without a specific set-aside. These organizations provide youth with parenting skills, including

---

[35] Prior the enactment of P.L. 110-378, states could receive a minimum of $100,000 and territories could receive a minimum of $45,000.

[36] This term means circumstances in which a youth would benefit to an unusual extent from additional time in the program. A youth in a TLP who has not reached age 18 on the last day of the 635-day period may, in exceptional circumstances and if otherwise qualified for the program, remain in the program until his or her 18th birthday.

child development education, family budgeting, health and nutrition, and other skills to promote their well-being and the well-being of their children.

Street Outreach Program[37]

(42 U.S.C. §5712d) Runaway and homeless youth living on the streets or in areas that increase their risk of using drugs or being subjected to sexual abuse, prostitution, or sexual exploitation are eligible to receive services through the Street Outreach Program. The program's goal is to assist youth in transitioning to safe and appropriate living arrangements. SOP services include outreach and education, treatment, counseling, provision of information, and referrals to other social service agencies. The Street Outreach Program is funded separately from the BCP and TLP, and is authorized to receive such sums as may be necessary. Since FY1996, when funding for the Street Outreach Program was established, community-based public and private organizations have been eligible to apply for SOP grants. Grants are generally awarded for a three-year period. Applicants may apply for a $100,000 grant each year for a maximum of $200,000 over that period. Most youth contacted through the Street Outreach Program receive written materials about referral services, health and hygiene products, and food and drink items.

Collaboration on the Prevention of Adolescent Dating Violence

The Family Violence Prevention and Services Act (FVPSA), Title III of the Child Abuse Amendments of 1984 (P.L. 98-457), authorized funds for Family Violence Prevention and Service grants that work to prevent family violence, improve service delivery to address family violence, and increase knowledge and understanding of family violence. Some of these projects focus on runaway and homeless youth in dating violence situations through HHS's Domestic Violence/Runaway and Homeless Youth Collaboration on the Prevention of Adolescent Dating Violence initiative. The initiative was created because many runaway and homeless youth come from homes where domestic violence occurs and may be at risk of abusing their partners or becoming victims of abuse.[38] The initiative funds projects carried out by faith-based and charitable organizations that advocate or provide direct services to runaway and homeless youth or victims of domestic violence. The grants fund training for staff at these organizations to enable them to assist youth in preventing dating violence. Eight projects are funded at $75,000 annually, for FY2008 through FY2010, the most recent funding cycle.

Department of Justice (DOJ)

Transitional Housing Assistance for Victims of Domestic Violence, Stalking, or Sexual Assault

(42 U.S.C. §13975) The 108th Congress passed the Prosecutorial Remedies and Other Tools to End the Exploitation of Children Today Act of 2003 (the PROTECT Act, P.L. 108-21), which

---

[37] This program is also known as the Education and Prevention Services to Reduce Sexual Abuse of Runaway, Homeless, and Street Youth Program.

[38] U.S. Department of Health and Human Services, Domestic Violence/Runaway and Homeless Youth Collaboration on the Prevention of Adolescent Dating Violence Grant Announcement, April 24, 2007, http://www.acf hhs.gov/grants/open/HHS-2007-ACF-ACYF-EV-0103 html.

contained the Transitional Housing Assistance for Victims of Domestic Violence, Stalking, or Sexual Assault program, and authorized it at $30 million per year through FY2008. Most recently, the Violence Against Women and Department of Justice Reauthorization Act of 2005 (P.L. 109-162) increased the authorized funding level for the transitional housing program, authorizing $40 million through FY2011. For more information about the Violence Against Women Act, see CRS Report R42499, *The Violence Against Women Act: Overview, Legislation, and Federal Funding*, by Lisa M. Seghetti and Jerome P. Bjelopera.

The PROTECT Act authorizes the Attorney General to provide grants to states, units of local governments, Indian tribes, and nonprofit organizations to assist eligible adults, minors, and their dependents who are fleeing domestic violence, or for whom emergency shelter services are lacking. Under the act, eligible adults, minors, and their dependents may be assisted with transitional housing, short-term housing assistance such as help with rent and utility payments, and supportive services, including help in finding and maintaining permanent housing. Grants may be used to help eligible persons with temporary housing for a maximum of 24 months. At least 7% of the total appropriation in any fiscal year for this program must be allocated to tribal organizations serving victims of domestic and dating violence, stalking, or sexual assault. For FY2005 through FY2011, Congress appropriated funding for the program through a set-aside from the STOP (Services, Training, Officers, and Prosecutors) grant. For FY2012, Congress appropriated and increased funding for the program separate from the STOP grant as part of the Consolidated and Further Continuing Appropriations Act (P.L. 112-55).

Department of Housing and Urban Development (HUD)

Homeless Assistance Grants

The Homeless Assistance Grants were established in 1987 as part of the Stewart B. McKinney Homeless Assistance Act (P.L. 100-77). The grants, administered by HUD, fund housing and services for homeless persons. The Homeless Assistance Grants have gone through several permutations since their enactment, with the most recent change taking place when the grants were reauthorized in the 111th Congress by the Homeless Emergency Assistance and Rapid Transition to Housing (HEARTH) Act, enacted as part of the Helping Families Save Their Homes Act (P.L. 111-22).

Until enactment of the HEARTH Act, the Homeless Assistance Grants were made up of four programs: the Emergency Shelter Grants (ESG) program, Supportive Housing Program (SHP), the Section 8 Moderate Rehabilitation Assistance for Single-Room Occupancy Dwellings (SRO) program, and the Shelter Plus Care (S+C) program. The HEARTH Act maintained the ESG program, but renamed it the Emergency Solutions Grants program, and consolidated the three remaining programs (SHP, SRO, and S+C), sometimes referred to as the "competitive grants," into one program called the "Continuum of Care" program (CoC). Funds appropriated for the ESG program will continue to be distributed via formula to states and localities while funds for the new CoC program, like its three predecessor programs, will be distributed through a competition.

The HEARTH Act specified that the provisions in the law would be effective on the earlier of 18 months from the law's enactment (on or about November 20, 2010) or three months from the date on which HUD publishes final regulations. Because HUD has not published final regulations for the CoC program, the changes in the HEARTH Act technically took effect 18 months after enactment. However, HUD has stated that current regulations apply until new regulations become effective, and FY2011 competitive funding was still distributed through the SHP, SRO, and S+C programs. As a result, this section of the report describes the ESG, SHP, SRO, and S+C programs because the CoC program has not yet been implemented. (To read more about changes that will occur when provisions of the HEARTH Act are implemented, see CRS Report RL33764, *The HUD Homeless Assistance Grants: Current Operation and HEARTH Act Changes*, by Libby Perl.)

Emergency Solutions Grants (ESG) Program

(42 U.S.C. §§11371-11378) The ESG program distributes formula grants to state and local governments; recipient governments may then distribute all or a portion of the funds to private nonprofit organizations that provide assistance to homeless individuals. ESG funds are distributed so that state and local governments receive the same proportion of total ESG funds as they receive of Community Development Block Grant (CDBG) funds. Factors used to determine how CDBG funds are distributed include poverty rates, population, the number of persons in poverty, housing overcrowding (homes in which there are more than 1.01 persons per room), the age of housing (the number of housing structures built prior to 1940), and the extent of population growth lag in a given community. There is a dollar-for-dollar match requirement for local governments; there is no match requirement for the first $100,000 for states but a dollar-for-dollar match is required for the remainder of the funds. Recipient states and local governments may use up to 7.5% of their grants for administrative costs.

ESG funds may be used in two categories: (1) emergency shelter and related services, and (2) homelessness prevention and rapid rehousing. The statute limits use of funds in the first category to the greater of 60% of a state or local government's ESG allocation or the amount the recipient spent for these purposes in the year prior to the effective date of the HEARTH Act.

- In the case of emergency shelter, funds may be used for the renovation, major rehabilitation, or conversion of buildings into emergency shelters. In addition, ESG funds may be used to provide services in conjunction with emergency shelter, including employment, health, or education services; family support services for homeless youth; substance abuse services; victim services; or mental health services. Another allowable use of funds is the maintenance, operation, insurance, utilities, and furnishing costs for these emergency shelters.

- Funds may also be used to prevent homelessness or to quickly find housing for those who find themselves homeless. Recipients may use funds to provide short- or medium-term rental assistance for individuals and families at risk of homelessness. Funds may also be used to provide services for those who are homeless or to help stabilize those at risk of homelessness. These services include housing searches, outreach to property owners, legal services, credit repair, payment of security or utility deposits, utility payments, a final month of rental assistance, or moving costs.

Supportive Housing Program (SHP)

(SHP was formerly codified at 42 U.S.C. §§11381-11389) Housing funded under the SHP may be transitional housing for individuals and families for up to 24 months, permanent housing for individuals with disabilities, or single room occupancy dwellings. In order to receive funds, permanent housing must provide supportive services for its residents such as case management, child care, employment assistance, outpatient health services, and food and cash assistance. States, local governmental entities, private nonprofit organizations, or community mental health associations that are public nonprofit organizations may apply for funds through their local Continuum of Care (CoC) planning boards. SHP requires that not less than 25% of funds be used to serve homeless families with children, not less than 25% be used to serve homeless persons with disabilities, and not less than 10% be used for providing supportive services. There is also a dollar-for-dollar match requirement for acquisition, rehabilitation, and construction activities, a 20% match for services, and a 25% match requirement for operational expenses. No provider may use more than 5% of SHP funds for administrative purposes.

Shelter Plus Care Program (S+C)

(S+C was formerly codified at 42 U.S.C. §§11403-11406b) The S+C program provides tenant- and project-based rental subsidies to homeless adults with disabilities. Like the Section 8 program, tenants pay 30% of their income toward housing and the administering body pays the rest. The assistance is initially funded for five years, but can be renewed at the end of those five years on an annual basis. S+C grants must be matched by local communities dollar for dollar. While S+C grant dollars cannot be used to fund supportive services, grantees are expected to partner with other agencies to provide services and the dollar for dollar match requirement can be met through spending on services. Not less than 50% of S+C rental units must be reserved for homeless individuals who are seriously mentally ill, have chronic substance abuse problems, or both. A state, unit of general local government (city, county, town, township, parish, or village), or public housing authority may apply for funds through their local CoC boards. Grantees may provide rental assistance to private nonprofit entities (including community mental health centers established as nonprofit organizations) that own or lease dwelling units.

Section 8 Moderate Rehabilitation Assistance for Single-Room Occupancy Dwellings (SRO)

(SRO was formerly codified at 42 U.S.C. §§11401, 11407-11407b) Under the SRO program, HUD provides rental subsidies, through public housing authorities, to support housing units that are similar to dormitories, having single bedrooms, community bathrooms, and kitchen facilities. The SRO units are funded as part of HUD's Section 8 Moderate Rehabilitation program; the program requires grant recipients to spend at least $3,000 per unit to rehabilitate property to be used for SRO housing. Grant recipients are then reimbursed for the costs of rehabilitating the SRO units through Section 8 rental assistance payments that they receive over a 10-year contract period. The costs of rehabilitation are amortized and added to a base rental amount.

Department of Labor (DOL)

Homeless Veterans Reintegration Program

(38 U.S.C. §2021) The Homeless Veterans Reintegration Program (HVRP) provides grants to states or other public entities and nonprofit organizations to operate employment programs that reach out to homeless veterans. The main goal of the HVRP is to reintegrate homeless veterans into the economic mainstream and labor force. HVRP grantee organizations provide services that include outreach, assistance in drafting a resume and preparing for interviews, job search

assistance, subsidized trial employment, job training, and follow-up assistance after placement. Recipients of HVRP grants also provide supportive services not directly related to employment such as transportation, provision of or assistance in finding housing, and referral for mental health treatment or substance abuse counseling. HVRP grantees often employ formerly homeless veterans to provide outreach to homeless veterans and to counsel them as they search for employment and stability. In 2010, the Veterans' Benefits Act of 2010 (P.L. 111-275) created a separate HVRP for women veterans and veterans with children. The new program, which includes child care among its services, is authorized from FY2011 through FY2015 at $1 million per year. In program year 2010, DOL awarded 26 grants to assist women veterans, totaling more than $5 million.[39]

HVRP, initially authorized as part of the McKinney Vento Homeless Assistance Act, was most recently authorized at $50 million through FY2012 as part of the Veterans Health Care Facilities Capital Improvement Act of 2011 (P.L. 112-37). (For more information about HVRP and other programs for homeless veterans, see CRS Report RL34024, *Veterans and Homelessness*, by Libby Perl.)

Referral and Counseling Services: Veterans at Risk of Homelessness Who Are Transitioning from Certain Institutions

(38 U.S.C. §2023) The Homeless Veterans Comprehensive Assistance Act of 2001 (P.L. 107-95) instituted a demonstration program to provide job training and placement services to veterans leaving prison, long-term care, or mental institutions who are at risk of homelessness. The enacting law gave both the VA and the Department of Labor authority over the program. By 2005, the program awarded $1.45 million in initial grants to seven recipients. These grants were extended through March 2006 with funding of $1.6 million and then again for an additional 15 months, through June 30, 2007, with $2 million in funding.[40] The statute enacting the program provided that it would cease on January 24, 2006, four years after its enactment. However, on October 10, 2008, Congress extended the program through FY2012 as part of the Veterans' Mental Health and Other Care Improvements Act of 2008 (P.L. 110-387). The new law removed the program's demonstration status and expanded the number of sites able to provide services to 12. In FY2011, the VA extended grants to 16 recipients to assist transitioning veterans.[41]

Department of Veterans Affairs (VA)

For more detailed information about VA programs for homeless veterans, see CRS Report RL34024, *Veterans and Homelessness*, by Libby Perl.

---

[39] U.S. Department of Labor, "US Labor Department announces more than $5 million in grants to organizations serving homeless female veterans and veterans with families," press release, June 20, 2010, http://www.dol.gov/opa/media/press/vets/VETS20100917 htm.

[40] U.S. Department of Labor, Office of the Assistance Secretary for Veterans' Employment and Training, *FY2006 and FY2007 Annual Report to Congress*, May 21, 2008, p. 12, http://www.dol.gov/vets/media/FY2006-2007_Annual_Report_To_Congress.pdf.

[41] U.S. Department of Labor, *FY2013 Congressional Budget Justifications*, p. VETS-44, http://www.dol.gov/dol/budget/2013/PDF/CBJ-2013-V3-05.pdf.

Health Care for Homeless Veterans (HCHV)[42]

(38 U.S.C. §§2031-2034) The Health Care for Homeless Veterans program operates at VA sites around the country where staff provide outreach services, physical and psychiatric health exams, treatment, and referrals to homeless veterans with mental health and substance use issues. As appropriate, the HCHV program places homeless veterans needing long-term treatment into one of its contract community-based facilities. Housing is provided either through residential treatment facilities that contract with the VA or through organizations that receive Grant and Per Diem funding for transitional housing (the "Homeless Providers Grant and Per Diem Program" is described below). In FY2009, VA's 132 HCHV sites provided outreach, treatment, and referral services to just over 77,696 homeless veterans.[43] Of those receiving assistance, 2,472 veterans stayed in residential treatment facilities in FY2009, with an average stay of about 68 days.[44] The HCHV program was most recently authorized through December 31, 2012, as part of the Veterans Health Care Facilities Capital Improvement Act of 2011 (P.L. 112-37).

Homeless Providers Grant and Per Diem Program[45]

(38 U.S.C. §§2011-2013) The Grant and Per Diem program has two aspects: the grants portion of the program funds capital grants that organizations may use to build or rehabilitate facilities to be used for transitional housing and service centers for homeless veterans, while the per diem portion funds services to homeless veterans. Specifically, capital grants may be used to purchase buildings, to expand or remodel existing buildings, and to procure vans for use in outreach to and transportation for, homeless veterans. Service centers for veterans must provide health care, mental health services, hygiene facilities, benefits and employment counseling, meals, transportation assistance, job training and placement services, and case management. The capital grants will fund up to 65% of the costs of acquisition, expansion, or remodeling of facilities, and grantees must provide the remaining 35%. Under the per diem portion of the program, both capital grant recipients and those organizations that would be eligible for capital grants (but have not applied for them) are eligible to apply for funds, although grant recipients have priority in receiving per diem funds.

The Grant and Per Diem program was most recently authorized as part of the Veterans Health Care Facilities Capital Improvement Act of 2011 (P.L. 112-37). The program had been permanently authorized at $150 million, but P.L. 112-37 increased the authorized levels for FY2010 ($175 million), FY2011 ($218 million), and FY2012 ($250 million) to comport with estimated obligation levels in the VA budget.[46] In FY2013 and thereafter, the authorized level returns to $150 million.

---

[42] Also known as the Homeless Chronically Mentally Ill Veterans (HCMI) program.

[43] Wesley J. Kasprow, Timothy Cuerdon, Diane DiLello, Leslie Cavallaro, and Nicole Harelik, *Healthcare for Homeless Veterans Programs: Twenty-Third Annual Report*, U.S. Department of Veterans Affairs Northeast Program Evaluation Center, March 25, 2010, p. 23.

[44] Ibid., pp. 121-122.

[45] Formerly called the Homeless Veterans Comprehensive Services Programs.

[46] U.S. Department of Veterans Affairs, *FY2012 Budget Submission, Volume II: Medical Programs and Information Technology*, pp. 1H-12, http://www.va.gov/budget/docs/summary/Fy2012_Volume_II-Medical_Programs_Information_Technology.pdf.

Homeless Veterans with Special Needs

(38 U.S.C. §2061) Within the Homeless Providers Grant and Per Diem program there is also a special purpose program that provides grants to health care facilities and to grant and per diem providers to encourage the development of programs for homeless veterans who are women (including women who care for minor dependents), frail elderly, terminally ill, or chronically mentally ill. The program was most recently authorized at $5 million per year through FY2012 as part of the Veterans Health Care Facilities Capital Improvement Act of 2011 (P.L. 112-37).

Domiciliary Care for Homeless Veterans (DCHV)

(38 U.S.C. §1710(b)) The Domiciliary Care for Homeless Veterans program is a residential rehabilitation program specifically intended to meet the clinical needs of homeless veterans while preventing the therapeutically inappropriate use of hospital and nursing home care services. Veterans served through the Domiciliary Care program typically suffer from mental illness, substance use disorders, or both.[47] The VA operates the DCHV program at 42 locations with 2,146 total beds across the country.[48] A multi-dimensional, individually tailored treatment approach is used to stabilize the clinical status of veterans while the underlying causes of homelessness are addressed. The basic components of the DCHV program include community outreach and referral, admission screening and assessment, medical and psychiatric evaluation, treatment and rehabilitation, and post-discharge community support. DCHV staff help veterans apply for housing assistance, or arrangements are made for placement of homeless veterans in long-term care facilities such as State Soldiers Homes, group homes, adult foster care, or halfway houses. Homeless veterans are provided employment training through involvement in the VA's Incentive Therapy Program, a medically prescribed rehabilitation program involving therapeutic work assignments at VA medical centers for which veterans receive nominal payments. In FY2009, 6,311 veterans completed treatment in DCHV programs with an average stay of 112 days at the VA facilities.[49]

Compensated Work Therapy Program[50]

(38 U.S.C. §2063) The Compensated Work Therapy (CWT) program is a comprehensive rehabilitation program that prepares veterans for competitive employment and independent living. The program was created by the Veterans Omnibus Health Care Act of 1976 (P.L. 94-581). The major goals of the program are (1) to use remunerative work to maximize a veteran's level of functioning; (2) to prepare veterans for successful re-entry into the community as productive citizens; and (3) to provide structured daily activity to those veterans with severe and chronic disabling physical and/or mental conditions. As part of their work therapy, veterans produce items for sale or undertake subcontracts to provide certain products and/or services such as temporary staffing to a company. Funds collected from the sale of these products and/or services are used to fund the program. Funding for this program comes from the VA's Special Therapeutic and

---

[47] Catherine Leda Seibyl, Sharon Medak, Linda Baldino, and Timothy Cuerdon, *Twenty-First Progress Report on the Domiciliary Care for Homeless Veterans Program, FY2009*, U.S. Department of Veterans Affairs Northeast Program Evaluation Center, March 24, 2010, p. 8.

[48] Ibid., p. 2.

[49] Ibid., pp. 7, 9.

[50] The CWT program was formerly called the Special Therapeutic and Rehabilitation Activities Fund.

Rehabilitation Activities Fund, and the program is permanently authorized at 38 U.S.C. Section 1718(c).

HUD VA Supported Housing (HUD-VASH)

(42 U.S.C. §1437f(o)(19)) HUD-VASH is a joint HUD and VA initiative that provides specially designated Section 8 rental assistance vouchers to homeless veterans while the VA provides supportive services. The HUD-VASH statute requires that the program serve homeless veterans who have chronic mental illnesses or chronic substance use disorders; however, this requirement has been waived in recent years. Every homeless veteran who receives a housing voucher must be assigned to a VA case manager and receive supportive services. Today's HUD-VASH program originally began as a Memorandum of Agreement between HUD and the VA, and through that relationship 1,780 vouchers were allocated to homeless veterans. The Homeless Veterans Comprehensive Assistance Act of 2001 (P.L. 107-95) codified the program and authorized the creation of an additional 500 vouchers each year for FY2003-FY2006. In the 109th Congress, the Veterans Benefits, Health Care, and Information Technology Act of 2006 (P.L. 109-461) similarly authorized additional HUD-VASH vouchers for FY2007 through FY2011.

Funds were not provided for additional vouchers until the 110th Congress, when the FY2008 Consolidated Appropriations Act (P.L. 110-161) allocated $75 million for additional HUD-VASH vouchers. This appropriation funded approximately 10,000 vouchers for one year (after the first year, vouchers are funded through the Section 8 account). Then, in both FY2009 and FY2010, Congress again appropriated $75 million for HUD-VASH (P.L. 111-8 and P.L. 111-117 respectively).[51] The appropriation for FY2011 was $50 million and funded approximately 6,800 vouchers (P.L. 112-10). The FY2012 appropriation went back up to $75 million, bringing the total number of vouchers available to nearly 48,000. Funds for supportive services are allocated through the VA health appropriation—VA budget documents estimated that obligations in FY2012 would be approximately $202 million.

Supportive Services for Veteran Families

In the 110th Congress, the Veterans' Mental Health and Other Care Improvements Act of 2008 (P.L. 110-387) authorized a program of supportive services to assist very low-income veterans and their families who either are making the transition from homelessness to housing or who are moving from one location to another. The VA calls the program Supportive Services for Veteran Families. The law specified that funds be made available for the program from the amount appropriated for VA medical services—$15 million for FY2009, $20 million for FY2010, and $25 million for FY2011. Most recently, the program was authorized for FY2012 at $100 million as part of the Veterans Health Care Facilities Capital Improvement Act of 2011 (P.L. 112-37).

On July 26, 2011, the VA announced the first round of funding for the SSVF grants.[52] A total of $60 million was awarded through a competitive process to 85 private nonprofit organizations and

---

[51] Nearly all of the HUD-VASH vouchers are made available to individual veterans to find housing in the private market. However, nearly 700 of the FY2010-funded vouchers and 100 of the FY2011-funded vouchers were distributed competitively to public housing authorities (PHAs) to be "project based." Project-basing of Section 8 vouchers occurs when a PHA decides to use the vouchers for particular units of housing rather than to maintain their portability.

[52] U.S. Department of Veterans Affairs, "VA Launches New Prevention Initiative to Serve 22,000 Veteran Families at Risk of Homelessness," press release, July 26, 2011, http://www.va.gov/opa/pressrel/pressrelease.cfm?id=2139.

consumer cooperatives, the entities that are to provide supportive services. Organizations that assist families transitioning from homelessness were given priority for funding. Among the eligible services that recipient organizations may provide are case management, health care services, daily living services, assistance with financial planning, transportation, legal assistance, child care, and housing counseling.

HUD and VA Homelessness Prevention Demonstration Program

As part of the FY2009 Omnibus Appropriations Act (P.L. 111-8), Congress appropriated $10 million through the HUD Homeless Assistance Grants Account to be used for a pilot program to prevent homelessness among veterans. The appropriation law required that the program be operated in a limited number of sites, at least three of which were to have a large number of individuals transitioning from military to civilian life, and up to four of which were to be in rural areas.

In July 2010, HUD issued a notice of implementation of the new demonstration program.[53] HUD, in consultation with the VA and DOL, selected five geographic areas in which local Continuums of Care (CoCs) are to assign a grantee to carry out the prevention program. The areas were chosen based on the number of homeless veterans reported by the local CoC and VA Medical Center, the number of Operation Iraqi Freedom and Operation Enduring Freedom veterans accessing VA health care, the presence and diversity of military sites in the area (e.g. representation of different branches of the military, National Guard, and Reserves), availability of VA health care, type of geographic area (urban versus rural), and the community's capacity to administer the prevention program. The five areas and corresponding military bases selected were (1) San Diego, CA (Camp Pendleton); (2) Killeen, TX (Fort Hood); (3) Watertown, NY (Fort Drum); (4) Tacoma, WA (Joint Base Lewis-McChord); and (5) Tampa, FL (MacDill Air Force Base).

The prevention program is to operate much like the Homelessness Prevention and Rapid Re-Housing Program created as part of the American Recovery and Reinvestment Act. Funds may be used for short-term rental assistance (up to three months) or medium-term rental assistance (4-18 months), for up to six months of rental arrears, for security or utility deposits, for utility payments, and for help with moving expenses.[54] Recipients may also use funds for supportive services that help veterans and their families find and maintain housing such as case management, housing search and placement, credit repair, child care, and transportation.[55]

Other Activities for Homeless Veterans

In addition to the targeted programs for which specific funding is available (see **Table 2** at the end of this report), the VA engages in several activities to assist homeless veterans that are not reflected in this report as separate programs. An Advisory Committee on Homeless Veterans was established within VA to consult with and seek advice concerning VA benefits and services to

---

[53] U.S. Department of Housing and Urban Development, *Notice of FY2009 Implementation of the Veterans Homelessness Prevention Demonstration Program*, July 14, 2010, http://www.hudhre.info/documents/ VetsHomelessPreventionDemo.pdf.

[54] Ibid., pp. 9-11.

[55] Ibid., p. 11.

homeless veterans (38 U.S.C. §2066). The Advisory Committee consists of 15 members appointed from Veterans Service Organizations, community-based homeless service providers, previously homeless veterans, experts in mental illness, substance use disorders, and others. The Advisory Committee was most recently authorized through December 30, 2012, as part of the Veterans Health Care Facilities Capital Improvement Act of 2011 (P.L. 112-37).

Another VA initiative is Comprehensive Homeless Centers (CHCs). These CHCs are located in eight cities, and consolidate all of the VA's homeless programs in that area into a single organizational framework to promote integration within the VA and coordination with non-VA homeless programs.[56] CHCs offer a comprehensive continuum of care to help homeless veterans escape from homelessness. The VA also sponsors Drop-in Centers, which provide a daytime sanctuary where homeless veterans can clean up, wash their clothes, get a daytime meal, and participate in a variety of low intensity therapeutic and rehabilitative activities. Linkages with longer-term assistance are also available. The VA Excess Property for Homeless Veterans Initiative provides for the distribution of federal excess personal property (hats, parkas, footwear, sleeping bags) to homeless veterans and homeless veterans programs.

The Department of Labor makes funds available through its Homeless Veterans Reintegration Program for local communities that organize Stand Downs for Homeless Veterans. Stand Downs are local events, staged annually in many cities across the country, in which local Veterans Service Organizations, businesses, government entities, and other social service organizations come together for up to three days to provide services for homeless veterans. Some of these services include food, shelter, clothing, and a range of other types of assistance, including VA provided health care, benefits certification, and linkages with other programs. Another program, called Veterans Benefits Administration's (VBA's) Acquired Property Sales for Homeless Providers, allows the VA to sell, at a discount, foreclosed properties to nonprofit organizations and government agencies that will use them to shelter or house homeless veterans. Finally, Project CHALENG for Veterans is a nationwide VA initiative to work with other agencies and better coordinate the response to the needs of homeless veterans. VA regional offices designate "points of contact" from among local service providers, and they in turn work with other federal agencies, state and local governments, and nonprofit organizations to assess the needs of homeless veterans and develop action plans to meet identified needs.

Social Security Administration (SSA)

The *SOAR Initiative (SSI/SSDI Outreach, Access and Recovery)*, while not a Social Security Administration (SSA) program, assists homeless individuals in obtaining Social Security Disability Insurance (SSDI) and Supplemental Security Income (SSI) benefits. SOAR was created through a collaborative effort among HHS, HUD, and SSA. SOAR makes technical assistance available to train state and local human services workers to better serve homeless individuals with mental illnesses or substance use disorders who may qualify for Social Security benefits. The program came about through the Homeless Policy Academy Initiative, a series of collaborations among HUD, HHS, VA, DOL, ED, the Interagency Council on Homelessness, and the states that took place from 2001 through 2007. SOAR was undertaken after multiple states requested training regarding the SSDI and SSI application processes.[57] As part of the initiative,

---

[56] Comprehensive Homeless Centers are located in Anchorage, Brooklyn, Cleveland, Dallas, Little Rock, Pittsburgh, San Francisco, and Los Angeles.

[57] U.S. Department of Health and Human Services, *Homeless Policy Academy Initiative: Final Contractors Report*, (continued...)

representatives from 34 states received SOAR training between 2005 and 2007.[58] Funds through the PATH program (described earlier in this report) have been used to train providers in SOAR,[59] and the Substance Abuse and Mental Health Service Administration (SAMHSA) continues to fund technical assistance to SOAR programs.[60] Currently all states participate in SOAR.[61]

In 2011, 71% of SOAR-assisted SSI or SSDI applicants were approved for benefits.[62] Although data are limited on how homeless applicants for benefits otherwise fare on initial application, among those localities that collect data, approval rates range between 10% and 15%.[63] Of all disability applicants in 2009 (the most recent year SSA data are available), 30% were awarded benefits.[64] An earlier evaluation of SOAR programs in 19 states also found improved access to housing for some individuals who gained benefits, and cost savings for state public benefits programs.[65]

In addition to SOAR, the Social Security Administration funded an initiative to increase the access of homeless individuals to federal benefits through employee training, outreach to homeless persons, and assistance with applications—the *Homeless Outreach Projects and Evaluation (HOPE)* initiative. Congress provided $8 million per year for the HOPE initiative from FY2003 through FY2005, and SSA funded 41 HOPE projects throughout the country over three years, with awardees expected to gradually reduce their dependence on HOPE funding.[66] Through the HOPE initiative, recipient organizations conducted outreach to homeless individuals with disabling conditions and assisted them with filling out applications for benefits such as SSI and SSDI. The program also helped individuals find assistance for their other needs, such as health care, counseling, and housing. An evaluation of the program found that, despite the fact that SSI and SSDI applications from HOPE program participants were processed more quickly than comparison groups, there was no significant difference in allowance rates between applications from HOPE programs and the comparison groups.[67] However, the evaluation found

---

(...continued)

April 2007, p. vi, http://www.hrsa.gov/homeless/pdf/finalreport.pdf.

[58] Initially, 24 states participated in SOAR training. In August 2007, an additional 10 states were selected to participate. See USICH Newsletter, August 9, 2007, http://www.ich.gov/newsletter/archive/08-09-07_e-newsletter.htm.

[59] See U.S. Department of Health and Human Services, *FY2011 Substance Abuse and Mental Health Services Administration Congressional Budget Justification*, p. SAMHSA/CMHS-57, http://www.samhsa.gov/Budget/FY2011/ SAMHSA_FY11CJ.pdf.

[60] Deborah Dennis, Margaret Lassiter, and William H. Connelly, et al., "Helping Adults Who Are Homeless Gain Disability Benefits: the SSI/SSDI Outreach, Access, and Recovery (SOAR) Program," *Psychiatric Services*, vol. 62, no. 11 (November 2011), pp. 1373-1374.

[61] Ibid.

[62] U.S. Department of Health and Human Services, Substance Abuse and Mental Health Services Administration, *2011 SOAR Outcomes*, February 2012, http://www.prainc.com/cms-assets/documents/52889-944292.2011-outcomes-summary-031212.pdf.

[63] Yvonne M. Perret, Deborah Dennis, and Margaret Lassiter, *Improving Social Security Disability Programs for Adults Experiencing Long-Term Homelessness*, National Academy of Social Insurance, November 14, 2008, p. 3, http://www.nasi.org/usr_doc/Perret_and_Dennis_January_2009_Rockefeller.pdf.

[64] Social Security Administration, *SSI Annual Statistical Report, 2010*, August 2011, Table 69, http://www.ssa.gov/ policy/docs/statcomps/ssi_asr/2010/ssi_asr10.pdf.

[65] *Preliminary Outcomes from the SOAR Technical Assistance Initiative*, Policy Research Associates, May 2008, http://www.prainc.com/SOAR/soar101/SOAROutcomes.pdf.

[66] For the funding announcement, see Social Security Administration, "Cooperative Agreements for Homeless Outreach Projects and Evaluation (HOPE)," 68 *Federal Register* 55698-55709, September 26, 2003.

[67] Marion L. McCoy, Cynthia S. Robins, James Bethel, Carina Tornow, and William D. Frey, *Evaluation of Homeless* (continued...)

---

improved housing conditions for HOPE program participants,[68] and that smaller percentages of participants were living on the streets, in shelters, or in places not meant for human habitation 12 months after participating in HOPE.

Current Issues

The Economic Downturn and Family Homelessness

In December 2008, the National Bureau of Economic Research declared that the economy had been in a recession since December 2007.[69] Although the end of the recession was determined to be June 2009,[70] the effects of an economic downturn continue to be seen in the employment sector, where the unemployment rate has remained above 8% since February of 2009, compared to 4.9% in December 2007.[71] The housing sector has also faced difficulty, with the foreclosure rate for all loans rising from 1.28% in the first quarter of 2007 to 4.39% in the first quarter of 2012.[72]

Increased foreclosures and rising unemployment may result in higher rates of homelessness among all groups, but particularly among families facing increased financial strain. For example, school districts reported an increase in the number of students who qualify for services under the Department of Education's definition of homelessness from nearly 679,724 during the 2006-2007 school year to 939,903 during the 2009-2010 school year.[73] The number of homeless students had increased for three years, through the 2008-2009 school year, when it reached 956,914 students. In June 2011, HUD released the *2010 Annual Homeless Assessment Report to Congress* (AHAR).[74] The report estimated the number of sheltered homeless people (those living in emergency or transitional housing) from October 2009 through September 2010. In 2010, an estimated 567,334 people in families (versus unaccompanied individuals[75]) experienced homelessness, an increase of 19.8% over the number in 2007.[76] The number of homeless

(...continued)

Outreach Projects and Evaluation (HOPE), Social Security Administration, October 2007, pp. 3-11 and 3-13, http://www.socialsecurity.gov/homelessness/docs/hopefinalreport.doc.

[68] Ibid., p. 3-15.

[69] National Bureau of Economic Research, *Determination of the December 2007 Peak in Economic Activity*, December 11, 2008, http://www.nber.org/cycles/dec2008.pdf.

[70] National Bureau of Economic Research, *Announcement of June 2009 Business Cycle Trough/End of Last Recession*, September 20, 2010, http://www.nber.org/cycles/sept2010.pdf.

[71] Unemployment rates taken from versions of the U.S. Department of Labor, Bureau of Labor Statistics, *The Employment Situation*. The most recent version is available at http://www.bls.gov/news.release/pdf/empsit.pdf.

[72] Mortgage Bankers Association, *National Delinquency Survey, First Quarter 2007*, data as of March 31, 2007, p. 3, and *National Delinquency Survey, First Quarter 2012*, data as of March 31, 2012, p. 3.

[73] National Center for Homeless Education, *Education for Homeless Children and Youths Program: Data Collection Summary*, June 2010, p. 8, http://center.serve.org/nche/downloads/data_comp_06-08.doc; and June 2011, p. 11, http://www2.ed.gov/programs/homeless/sy2009ehcy.doc.

[74] U.S. Department of Housing and Urban Development, *2010 Annual Homeless Assessment Report to Congress*, June 2011, http://www.hudhre.info/documents/2010HomelessAssessmentReport.pdf (hereinafter, 2010 AHAR).

[75] HUD includes unaccompanied adults, unaccompanied youth, and multi-adult households without children in its estimate of unaccompanied individuals.

[76] 2010 AHAR, pp. 11-12.

households with children in 2010 was estimated to be 168,227, an increase of 28.4% over the number of households with children estimated to be homeless in 2007 (130,968).[77] Unaccompanied individuals still continue to make up the largest percentage of people experiencing homelessness, representing 65.5% of those who were estimated to be homeless in the 2010 AHAR.[78] However, homelessness among sheltered single individuals was estimated to have fallen by 6.4% from 2007 to 2010.[79]

Efforts to End Homelessness

More than a decade ago, the concept of ending homelessness was introduced in a report from the National Alliance to End Homelessness (NAEH), which outlined a strategy to end homelessness in 10 years.[80] The plan included four recommendations: developing local, data-driven plans to address homelessness; using mainstream programs (such as TANF, Section 8, and SSI) to prevent homelessness; employing a housing first strategy to assist most people who find themselves homeless; and developing a national infrastructure of housing, income, and service supports for low-income families and individuals. While the idea of ending homelessness for all people was embraced by many groups, the Bush Administration and federal government focused on ending homelessness among chronically homeless individuals specifically. For most of the decade, the term chronically homeless was defined as "an unaccompanied homeless individual with a disabling condition who has been continually homeless for a year or more, or has had at least four episodes of homelessness in the past three years."[81] The HEARTH Act updated the definition to include families with a head of household who has a disability.[82]

In the year following the release of the NAEH report, then-HUD Secretary Martinez announced HUD's commitment to ending chronic homelessness at the NAEH annual conference. In 2002, as a part of his FY2003 budget, President Bush made "ending chronic homelessness in the next decade a top objective." The bipartisan, congressionally mandated Millennial Housing Commission, in its Report to Congress in 2002, included ending chronic homelessness in 10 years among its principal recommendations.[83] And by 2003, the United States Interagency Council on Homelessness (USICH) had been re-engaged after six years of inactivity and was charged with pursuing the President's 10-year plan.[84] For the balance of the decade, multiple federal initiatives focused funding and efforts on this goal.

However, the initiative to end chronic homelessness has raised some concerns among advocates for homeless people that allocating resources largely to chronically homeless individuals is done

---

[77] Ibid. p. 11.

[78] Ibid.

[79] Ibid., pp. 11-12.

[80] National Alliance to End Homelessness, *A Plan: Not a Dream. How to End Homelessness in Ten Years*, June 1, 2000, http://www.endhomelessness.org/files/585_file_TYP_pdf.pdf.

[81] 24 C.F.R. §91.5. The Homeless Emergency Assistance and Rapid Transition to Housing (HEARTH) Act (P.L. 111-22) changed the definition to include families with an adult member who has a disabling condition.

[82] 42 U.S.C. §11360(2).

[83] The report is available at http://govinfo.library.unt.edu/mhc/MHCReport.pdf. See pp. 54-56.

[84] The Interagency Council on Homelessness (ICH) was created in 1987 in the Stewart B. McKinney Homeless Assistance Act, P.L. 100-77. Its mission is to coordinate the national response to homelessness. The ICH is composed of the directors of 19 federal departments and agencies whose policies and programs have some responsibility for homeless services, including HUD, HHS, DOL, and the VA.

at the expense of families with children who are homeless, homeless youth, and other vulnerable populations.[85] The HEARTH Act mandated that the USICH draft a Federal Strategic Plan to End Homelessness among all groups (families with children, unaccompanied youth, veterans, and chronically homeless individuals) within a year of the law's enactment, and to update the plan annually. In addition to the USICH plan, in November 2010 the VA announced a plan to end homelessness among veterans within five years. These plans—to end chronic homelessness, to end homelessness generally, and to end veterans' homelessness—are described below.

The Chronic Homelessness Initiative

In 2002, the Bush Administration established a national goal of ending chronic homelessness within 10 years, by 2012. An impetus behind the initiative to end chronic homelessness is that chronically homeless individuals are estimated to account for about 10% of all users of the homeless shelter system, but are estimated to use nearly 50% of the total days of shelter provided.[86]

Permanent supportive housing is generally seen as a solution to ending chronic homelessness.[87] Permanent supportive housing consists of low-cost housing, paired with social services, available to low-income and/or homeless households. Services can include case management, substance abuse counseling, mental health services, income management and support, and life skills services. Providing permanent supportive housing to homeless adults with mental illnesses or substance abuse disorders is sometimes referred to as the "housing first" approach—housing is found for homeless individuals prior to treatment of their illnesses and addictions. In the late 1990s, research began to show that finding housing for homeless individuals with severe mental illnesses meant that they were less likely to be housed temporarily by more expensive public services, such as hospitals, jails, or prisons.[88]

More recently, two studies have examined outcomes of housing first initiatives. A study published in the *Journal of the American Medical Association* in 2009 examined outcomes among residents in a development for chronically homeless individuals with severe alcohol problems living in Seattle.[89] Many residents had been high-cost users of emergency room services, sobriety centers, and jails. Researchers found that the total costs of serving residents in the 12 months prior to their moving into the housing development (including shelter nights, time in jail, emergency medical

---

[85] See, for example, the House Financial Services Committee, Subcommittee on Housing and Community Opportunity, *Hearing on Reauthorization of the McKinney-Vento Homeless Assistance Act, Part II*, 110th Cong., 2nd sess., October 16, 2007, http://frwebgate.access.gpo.gov/cgi-bin/getdoc.cgi?dbname=110_house_hearings&docid=f:39908.pdf.

[86] Randall Kuhn and Dennis Culhane, "Applying Cluster Analysis to Test a Typology of Homelessness by Pattern of Shelter Utilization: Results from the Analysis of Administrative Data," *American Journal of Community Psychology*, vol. 26, no. 2 (April 1998), p. 219.

[87] Report from the Secretary's Work Group on Ending Chronic Homelessness, *Ending Chronic Homelessness: Strategies for Action*, Department of Health and Human Services, March 2003, pp. 12-13, http://aspe.hhs.gov/hsp/homelessness/strategies03/.

[88] See Dennis Culhane, Stephen Metraux, and Trevor Hadley, "Public Service Reductions Associated with Placement of Homeless Persons with Severe Mental Illness in Supportive Housing," *Housing Policy Debate*, vol. 13, no. 1 (2002): 107-163.

[89] Mary E. Larimer, Daniel K. Malone, and Michelle D. Garner, et al., "Health Care and Public Service Use and Costs Before and After Provision of Housing for Chronically Homeless Persons with Severe Alcohol Problems," *Journal of the American Medical Association*, vol. 301, no. 13 (April 1, 2009), pp. 1349-1357.

services, and Medicaid and other healthcare costs) were $42,964 per person per year.[90] Twelve months after moving into the development, the cost had been reduced to $13,440 per resident per year. Cost reductions grew over time, indicating that length of time housed could contribute to savings.[91] In addition, the median number of drinks consumed by residents per day and days drinking to intoxication also declined.[92] A HUD study published in 2007 looked at housing stability and health outcomes of residents in three housing first programs. During a one-year period, 43% of clients in the three programs remained in housing during the entire 12-month period while another 41% stayed intermittently, ultimately returning to the housing first programs before the end of the year.[93] Regarding health outcomes, the study found little change in psychiatric impairment among those who stayed in housing permanently or intermittently and some decrease in participants' levels of impairment related to substance use.[94]

The Administration undertook several projects to reach its goal of ending chronic homelessness within 10 years, each of which took place during the mid-2000s. These included (1) a collaboration among HUD, HHS, and VA (the *Collaborative Initiative to Help End Chronic Homelessness*) that funded housing and treatment for chronically homeless individuals; (2) a HUD and DOL project called *Ending Chronic Homelessness through Employment and Housing*, through which HUD funded permanent supportive housing and DOL offered employment assistance; and (3) a HUD pilot program called *Housing for People Who Are Homeless and Addicted to Alcohol* that provided supportive housing for chronically homeless persons.

In addition, since FY2005 HUD has encouraged the development of housing for chronically homeless individuals in the way that it distributes the Homeless Assistance Grants to applicants through its annual grant competition. HUD awards points to applicants if their Continuums of Care (the geographic entities that collectively apply to HUD for funds) have developed 10-year plans to end chronic homelessness. In addition, through the competition grantees can receive additional funding—a "permanent housing bonus"—if they create permanent supportive housing for individuals with disabilities or families with an adult member who has a disability. While the permanent housing bonus does not technically require that housing be created for those who are chronically homeless, often those homeless individuals who have disabilities are chronically homeless. Prior to 2009, the permanent housing bonus was available only to develop housing for chronically homeless individuals.

When the Continuum of Care program authorized by the HEARTH Act is implemented, at least 30% of funds (not including those for permanent housing renewal contracts) are to be used to provide permanent supportive housing to individuals with disabilities or families with an adult head of household (or youth in the absence of an adult) who has a disability. This requirement will be reduced proportionately as communities increase permanent housing units for those individuals and families, and it will end when HUD determines that a total of 150,000 permanent housing units have been provided for homeless persons with disabilities since 2001.

---

[90] Ibid., p. 1355.

[91] Ibid., p. 1356.

[92] Ibid., pp. 1354-1355.

[93] Carol L. Pearson, Gretchen Locke, Ann Elizabeth Montgomery, and Larry Buron, *The Applicability of Housing First Models to Homeless Persons with Serious Mental Illness*, U.S. Department of Housing and Urban Development, July 2007, p. 62, http://www.huduser.org/Publications/pdf/hsgfirst.pdf. The sample size in the study was 80 individuals.

[94] Ibid., pp. 83-84 and 88-89.

The U.S. Interagency Council on Homelessness Federal Strategic Plan to Prevent and End Homelessness

The HEARTH Act, enacted on May 20, 2009, as part of the Helping Families Save Their Homes Act (P.L. 111-22), charged the U.S. Interagency Council on Homelessness (USICH) with developing a National Strategic Plan to End Homelessness. The HEARTH Act specified that the plan should be made available for public comment and submitted to Congress and the President within one year of the law's enactment. The USICH convened working groups made up of members of federal agencies to discuss ending homelessness among specific populations: families, youth, chronically homeless individuals, and veterans.[95] The council then held regional meetings to get feedback from various stakeholders, and it accepted public comments on its website during March 2010.[96]

On June 22, 2010, the USICH released their report entitled *Opening Doors*.[97] The plan sets out goals of ending chronic homelessness as well as homelessness among veterans within the next five years and ending homelessness for families, youth, and children within the next 10 years. The report lays out five overarching strategies to assist in accomplishing these goals; each category has between one and three specific objectives to pursue in furtherance of the goals. The five categories are (1) increasing leadership, collaboration, and civic engagement; (2) increasing access to stable and affordable housing; (3) increasing economic security; (4) improving health and stability; and (5) retooling the homeless crisis response.[98]

The 2011 update to *Opening Doors* reported on progress toward its goals by looking at the numbers of people experiencing homelessness, including subgroups (families with children, chronically homeless individuals, and veterans), the number of permanent supportive housing units available for homeless individuals, and the number of people experiencing homelessness who leave homeless assistance programs with either earned income or access to mainstream benefits.[99] The report presented data from HUD's point-in-time estimates of homelessness in 2010, which found increases in homelessness for families with children (1.5%) and veterans (1.0%), but a decrease among chronically homeless individuals (1.0%).[100] The permanent supportive housing inventory grew by more than 17,000 units from 2009 to 2010, from 219,381 to 236,798.[101] The USICH did not yet have 2010 data on earned income or mainstream benefits to compare to 2009 levels.

---

[95] U.S. Interagency Council on Homelessness, *Federal Strategic Plan to Prevent and End Homelessness Overview*, http://www.usich.gov/PDF/FSPOverviewSummary.pdf.

[96] For public comments, see http://fsp.uservoice.com/forums/41991-how-can-the-local-community-contribute-to-the-visi.

[97] U.S. Interagency Council on Homelessness, *Opening Doors: Federal Strategic Plan to Prevent and End Homelessness*, June 2010, http://www.ich.gov/PDF/OpeningDoors_2010_FSPPreventEndHomeless.pdf.

[98] Ibid., p 26.

[99] U.S. Interagency Council on Homelessness, *Opening Doors: Federal Strategic Plan to Prevent and End Homelessness, Update 2011*, 2012, http://www.usich.gov/resources/uploads/asset_library/USICH_FSPUpdate_2012_12312.pdf.

[100] Ibid., p. 20.

[101] Ibid., p. 21.

The Department of Veterans Affairs Plan to End Homelessness

On November 3, 2009, the VA announced a plan to end homelessness among veterans within five years.[102] However, the VA has not released a formal written plan, and instead, VA budget documents outline areas of focus for the new plan. At least two bills introduced in the 112ᵗʰ Congress call on the VA to submit plans to Congress: the Helping Homeless Heroes Act (H.R. 2559) and the Veterans Programs Improvement Act (S. 1148).

Beginning with the FY2011 budget, VA budget documents have outlined six areas of focus for ending homelessness. These are (1) outreach and education, (2) treatment, (3) prevention, (4) housing and supportive services, (5) employment and benefits, and (6) community partnerships.[103] In its FY2013 budget, the VA noted that it expected to continue expanding the number of veterans served through HUD-VASH, Healthcare for Homeless Veterans, the Grant and Per Diem Program, Supportive Services for Veteran Families, and other programs and initiatives.

Legislation in the 112ᵗʰ Congresses

Enacted Legislation

The Veterans Health Care Facilities Capital Improvement Act of 2011 (P.L. 112-37), approved by the House on September 20, 2011, and the Senate three days later, extended the expiring authorizations for a number of programs that assist homeless veterans, including the following:

- **Homeless Veterans Reintegration Program:** The authorization was extended from the end of FY2011 through the end of FY2012 at the previous authorization level ($50 million).

- **Health Care for Homeless Veterans Program:** The authorization was extended from December 31, 2011, through December 31, 2012.

- **Grant and Per Diem Program:** The program had been permanently authorized at $150 million. P.L. 112-37 increased the authorization for each year from FY2010 through FY2012. Levels were increased to $175 million, $218 million, and $250 million for each year, respectively. The higher authorization levels comport with amounts that the VA estimates are needed for the program in each of the three fiscal years.[104] Beginning in FY2013 and thereafter, the authorization level returns to $150 million.

- **Supportive Services for Veteran Families:** The authorization was extended through FY2012 at $100 million. The program had previously been authorized

---

[102] See U.S. Department of Veterans Affairs, "Secretary Shinseki Details Plan to End Homelessness for Veterans," press release, November 3, 2009, http://www1.va.gov/OPA/pressrel/pressrelease.cfm?id=1807.

[103] See, for example, *FY2013 VA Budget Justifications*, Volume 2 Medical Programs and Information Technology, p. 1I-15, http://www.va.gov/budget/docs/summary/Fy2013_Volume_II-Medical_Programs_Information_Technology.pdf.

[104] U.S. Department of Veterans Affairs, *FY2012 Budget Submission, Volume II: Medical Programs and Information Technology*, pp. 1H-12, http://www.va.gov/budget/docs/summary/Fy2012_Volume_II-Medical_Programs_Information_Technology.pdf.

---

for three years: FY2009 at $15 million, FY2010 at $20 million, and FY2011 at $25 million.

- **Grant and Per Diem Program for Homeless Veterans with Special Needs:** The authorization was extended through FY2012 and remained at the previous level ($5 million).

Active Legislation

Two bills that would reauthorize the Violence Against Women Act, both called the **Violence Against Women Reauthorization Act, S. 1925 and H.R. 4970**, have been passed by the Senate and House respectively. Both bills would reauthorize the program to provide transitional housing to those who are homeless as a result of domestic violence, and would rename it "Transitional Housing Assistance for Victims of Domestic Violence, Dating Violence, Sexual Assault, and Stalking."[105] The authorization level for the program would be $35 million per year from FY2012 through FY2016 (down from its previously authorized level of $40 million from FY2007 through FY2011). In addition, both S. 1925 and H.R. 4970 would define "qualified application" for grant funding in such a way to ensure that service providers do not conduct background checks or clinical evaluations of victims; have an understanding of domestic and dating violence, sexual assault, and stalking; and do not make services for victims mandatory. In addition, S. 1925 contains a provision not included in H.R. 4970 that would add to the eligible supportive services that grantees may provide to include those related to securing and retaining employment.

Also in the 112th Congress, legislation to reauthorize the Education for Homeless Children and Youth program as part of the reauthorization of Elementary and Secondary Education Act (ESEA) has been reported by both House and Senate committees. On October 20, 2011, the Senate Committee on Health, Education, Labor, and Pensions ordered reported a bill to reauthorize the ESEA, titled the Elementary and Secondary Education Reauthorization Act of 2011 (no bill number yet). Reauthorization of EHCY is included as part of this legislation. On February 28, 2012, the House Committee on Education and the Workforce ordered reported two bills to reauthorize portions of the ESEA. One of these bills is **H.R. 3990, the Encouraging Innovation and Effective Teachers Act**. Title VI of this bill would reauthorize EHCY. The other bill is **H.R. 3989, the Student Success Act**. It includes amendments to ESEA Title I-A that impact EHCY. For more information about reauthorization, see CRS Report R42494, *Education for Homeless Children and Youth: Background and Legislation in the 112th Congress*, by Gail McCallion.

The **Homeless Children and Youth Act of 2011 (H.R. 32)** was approved by the House Financial Services Committee, Subcommittee on Insurance, Housing, and Community Opportunity on February 7, 2012. The bill would broaden the McKinney-Vento Act definition of "homeless individual" by including children and their families and youth who have been verified as homeless under four other federal programs: Runaway and Homeless Youth, Education for Homeless Children and Youths, Head Start, and programs through the Individuals with Disabilities Education Act. H.R. 32 is also discussed in the section of this report entitled "Defining Homelessness: Who Is Served."

---

[105] The new definition would remove the word "child" from the title and add the term "dating violence."

The **Homes for Heroes Act of 2011 (H.R. 3298)** was passed by the House on March 27, 2012. The bill would create a position within HUD, the Special Assistant for Veterans Affairs, to act as a liaison to the VA and the Interagency Council on Homelessness, to coordinate all HUD programs and activities relating to veterans, and to ensure that veterans receive fair access to HUD housing and homeless assistance, among other activities. The bill would also require HUD and the VA to continue to coordinate in releasing the *Veterans Supplement to the Annual Homeless Assessment Report to Congress*, and to report information about veterans served through HUD-VASH, a description of whether and how veterans may be given special consideration in Public Housing Authority plans, HUD's cost of administering programs for veterans, and on the activities of the Special Assistant for Veterans Affairs.

Funding

Table 1 shows final appropriation levels for FY2005-FY2012 for the targeted homelessness programs included in this report with the exception of programs administered by the VA. The table also contains a column showing appropriations that were made as part of the American Recovery and Reinvestment Act (P.L. 111-5). The appropriations figures come from the budget justifications submitted by the various agencies or from congressional appropriations documents. **Table 2** shows actual obligations for the Department of Veterans Affairs targeted homeless programs for FY2004-FY2011 and estimated obligations for FY2012. The figures in **Table 2** were obtained from VA budget documents and conversations with VA employees.

Table 1. Homelessness: Appropriations for Targeted Federal Programs, FY2005-FY2012

(dollars in thousands)

Program	Agency	FY2005	FY2006	FY2007	FY2008	FY2009 Stimulus Act, P.L. 111-5	FY2009	FY2010	FY2011[a]	FY2012
Education for Homeless Children & Youth	ED	62,496	61,871[b]	61,871	64,067[c]	70,000	65,427	65,427	65,296	65,173
Emergency Food & Shelter	DHS/FEMA	153,000	151,470	151,470	153,000	100,000	200,000[d]	200,000[e]	119,760	120,000
Health Care for the Homeless[f]	HHS	149,000	151,400	167,900	174,700[c]	160,000[g]	171,700	171,300	199,000	214,000
Projects for Assistance in Transition from Homelessness	HHS	54,809	54,223	54,261	53,313[c]	—	59,687	65,047	64,917	64,917
Consolidated Runaway and Homeless Youth Program	HHS	88,725	87,777	87,837	96,128[c]	—	97,234	97,734	97,539	97,355
—Runaway and Homeless Youth—Basic Center	HHS	48,786	48,265	48,298	52,860	—	53,469	53,744	53,637	53,536
—Runaway and Homeless Youth—Transitional Living	HHS	39,939	39,511	39,539	43,268	—	43,765	43,990	43,902	43,819
Runaway and Homeless Youth Street Outreach Program	HHS	15,178	15,017	15,027	17,221[c]	—	17,721	17,971	17,935	17,901
Homeless Assistance Grants	HUD	1,240,511	1,326,600	1,441,600	1,585,990	—[h]	1,677,000	1,865,000	1,901,000	1,901,000
—Homelessness Prevention and Rapid Re-housing						1,500,000				
Homeless Veterans Reintegration Program	DOL	20,832	21,780	21,809	23,620[c]	—	26,330	36,330	36,257	38,185
Transitional Housing Assistance for Victims of Domestic Violence, Stalking, or Sexual Assault[i]	DOJ	12,333	14,808	14,847	17,390	50,000	18,000	18,000	17,964	25,000

Source: Table prepared by the Congressional Research Service (CRS). Unless otherwise stated, sources of data are agency budget justifications and congressional appropriations documents. The amounts are enacted values and do not necessarily include all rescissions for each program in each fiscal year.

Notes: Italics indicate amount is subsumed under earlier line item.

a. In FY2011, all discretionary accounts were subject to an across-the-board rescission of 0.2%. Unless otherwise noted, the funding levels in the table have been reduced by the rescission amount.

b. P.L. 109-148 provided supplemental FY2006 appropriations of $5 million for assistance to local educational agencies serving homeless children and youth who were displaced by Hurricane Katrina or Hurricane Rita.

c. In the FY2008 Consolidated Appropriations Act, P.L. 110-161, Division G, Section 528, an across-the-board rescission of 1.747% was applied to nearly all Departments of Labor, Health and Human Services, and Education programs. The values in the table reflect the rescission.

d. Funds for the Emergency Food and Shelter program were appropriated as part of the Consolidated Security, Disaster Assistance, and Continuing Appropriations Act (P.L. 110-329), while appropriations for the remaining programs were part of the FY2009 Omnibus Appropriations Act (P.L. 111-8).

e. In FY2010, funds for the Emergency Food and Shelter Program were appropriated as part of the Department of Homeland Security Appropriations Act (P.L. 111-83); all other programs received appropriations as part of the Consolidated Appropriations Act (P.L. 111-117).

f. The Health Care for the Homeless program is funded under the Health Resources and Services Administration (HRSA), Community Health Centers program. The law requires that health centers serving special populations, including homeless individuals, receive the same proportion of funds that they received in FY2001 (42 U.S.C. §254b(r)(2)(B)). For the Health Care for the Homeless program, this is approximately 8.6% of the funds appropriated for the Community Health Centers program. The appropriation estimate for FY2005 in the table is based on this figure. For FY2006 forward, CRS relied on the U.S. Department of Health and Human Services Moyer Materials.

g. The American Recovery and Reinvestment Act (ARRA, P.L. 111-5) appropriated $500 million for health centers to fund services to patients, as well as $1.5 billion in infrastructure funding for facility construction and renovation, the purchase of equipment, and acquisition of health information technology. According to HHS, $160 million went to serve homeless individuals. See U.S. Department of Health and Human Services, Office of the Assistant Secretary for Resources and Technology, *FY2012 Moyer Material*, April 2011, p. 30.

h. Although funds appropriated through ARRA for homelessness prevention and rapid re-housing were distributed using the Emergency Shelter Grants formula, the funds are administered according to different rules than those under the four existing Homeless Assistance Grants.

i. Until FY2012, funding was provided as a set-aside under the VAWA STOP grant program.

Table 2. Homelessness: Targeted VA Program Obligations, FY2004-FY2012

(dollars in thousands)

Program	FY2004	FY2005	FY2006	FY2007	FY2008	FY2009	FY2010	FY2011	FY2012 (estimate)
Health Care for Homeless Veterans (HCHV)[a]	42,905	40,357	56,998	71,925	77,656	80,219	109,727	200,808	134,738
Homeless Providers Grants and Per Diem Program[b]	62,965	62,180	63,621	81,187	114,696	128,073	175,057	148,097	194,477
Domiciliary Care for Homeless Veterans (DCHV)	51,829	57,555	63,592	77,633	96,098	115,373	175,979	221,938	201,304
Compensated Work Therapy/Therapeutic Residence Program (CWT/TR)	10,240	10,004	19,529	21,514	21,497	22,206	61,205	73,420	57,743
Services for HUD VA Supported Housing (HUD-VASH)	3,375	3,243	3,626	7,487	4,854	26,601	71,137	119,603	201,500
Supportive Services for Veteran Families[c]	—	—	—	—	—	218	3,881	60,541	100,000

Source: Department of Veterans Affairs budget documents.

a. Includes funding for the Homeless Chronically Mentally Ill Veterans (HCMI) and the Homeless Comprehensive Service Centers, including mobile centers. A specific breakdown of obligations among activities is not available.

b. Does not include funding for Grant and Per Diem Liaisons.

c. The first award for the Supportive Services for Veteran Families program was made in FY2011.

Author Contact Information

Libby Perl, Coordinator
Specialist in Housing Policy
eperl@crs.loc.gov, 7-7806

Erin Bagalman
Analyst in Health Policy
ebagalman@crs.loc.gov, 7-5345

Adrienne L. Fernandes-Alcantara
Specialist in Social Policy
afernandes@crs.loc.gov, 7-9005

Elayne J. Heisler
Analyst in Health Services
eheisler@crs.loc.gov, 7-4453

Gail McCallion
Specialist in Social Policy
gmccallion@crs.loc.gov, 7-7758

Francis X. McCarthy
Analyst in Emergency Management Policy
fmccarthy@crs.loc.gov, 7-9533

Key Policy Staff

Program	Name	Telephone and Email
Education for Homeless Children and Youths	Gail McCallion	7-7758 gmccallion@crs.loc.gov
Emergency Food and Shelter program	Francis X. McCarthy	7-9533 fmccarthy@crs.loc.gov
Health Centers for the Homeless	Elayne Heisler	7-4453 eheisler@crs.loc.gov
HUD programs and Homeless Veterans	Libby Perl	7-7806 eperl@crs.loc.gov
Projects for Assistance in Transition from Homelessness and SAMHSA Grants	Erin Bagalman	7-5345 ebagalman@crs.loc.gov
Runaway and Homeless Youth programs	Adrienne L. Fernandes-Alcantara	7-9005 afernandes@crs.loc.gov
Violence Against Women Act programs	Lisa Sacco	7-7359 lsacco@crs.loc.gov